Catastrophes

Catastrophes

DIAN TINIO

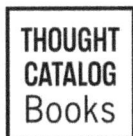

THOUGHT
CATALOG
Books

BROOKLYN, NY

THOUGHT
CATALOG
Books

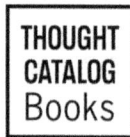

Published by Thought Catalog Books, a division of The Thought &
Expression Co., Williamsburg, Brooklyn. Founded in 2010, Thought
Catalog is a website and imprint dedicated to your ideas and stories.
We publish fiction and non-fiction from emerging and established
writers across all genres. For general information and submissions:
manuscripts@thoughtcatalog.com.

First edition, 2017

ISBN: 978-1945796548

Printed and bound in the United States.

10 9 8 7 6 5 4 3 2 1

To my Father—
I couldn't have done this without you.

For my father—
I hope I made you proud.

This is my whole heart. I hope you will be gentle with it.

Part 1

The Calm

1

I Hope You Stop Apologizing

I hope you stop apologizing for your heart. Stop apologizing for allowing that muscle inside you to feel deeply for places, experiences and souls. For permitting you to care for the people around you. For having compassion for the ones you encounter along the streets.

I hope you stop apologizing for your mind. For what you believe in, for your faith, for what you fight for, for your ideas. Stop apologizing for your questions or your opinions. As long as you said it with enough respect, you let it out. You express it, but you know that doesn't give you permission to step on the opinions of others. You respect theirs but you don't apologize for your own. You stand resilient. Because if you don't, you won't be able to stand for anything else.

I hope you stop apologizing for your choices. Only you can say if your choices affect you for better or for worse. Only you can allow these choices to destroy you. Let yourself make choices and boldly stand firm in them. Bad choices—charge it to experiences. Good choices—give yourself that friendly nod. There is no such thing as a wrong choice. Believe that every choice you make will direct you to a brighter future once you allow it to do its magic. You learn from bad choices, and if it doesn't benefit you, well, you don't make it again. You make a good choice and you're one step closer.

I hope you stop apologizing for your people. Stop defending the people you love. You love them for a reason and you hold on to that reason. You don't have to dress them up so they'll look better before critics. You don't need to say sorry for loving people too deeply and too sincerely. Nothing is more spectacular than loving someone unapologetically. Just continue; love them with all your heart. Allow yourself to fully trust and fully love.

I hope you stop apologizing for who you are. For the way you rise, the way you fall, the way you fight, the way you fail, the way you prevail. Kindly stop. You are made with so much beauty and bravery. Why do you always think you're weak and good for nothing? Why do you think you're a mistake? You have no purpose? You're full of purpose and you're worth all the love in the world. You are deserving. You are loved and incredible. Stop making way for lies in your heart. Let them fall by the wayside. Trust your spark; don't hide your light. You are meant to shine intensely.

2

Maybe

Maybe if we treat ourselves better we will learn not to allow anyone to disrespect us. Maybe if we give ourselves space to grow we will detach from anyone who belittle us. And maybe, just maybe, if we love ourselves more we will never settle for a love that is less.

3

You'll Never Find Yourself If You're Lost In Someone Else

Don't spend your key years falling desperately in love with everyone you meet. Don't be too consumed, too distracted loving these people. Don't let the way someone treats you typify your very worth. Don't be too caught up in loving them that you forgot how to love yourself right.

You're young, and if you spend your time figuring out your life with someone else, growing with them, merging your distinct personality with theirs, you'll never really know who you are.

Give yourself the opportunity to get to know yourself a little deeper. To find out the exact things that make you glad, the things you're undeniably passionate about, the things that makes you upset, the things you despise. Understand that you have to figure these things out on your own, without the influence of someone else. You need to curate who you are with full focus.

Your 20s are the time of your life when you'll truly be young, responsible, and independent. Explore your identity. Be your own person.

4

If You Can't Love Them Wholly, Let Them Go

Because somebody out there will.

If you can't bear to see how their hair looks like when they get out of bed in the morning, let them go. If it irritates you how they like hot chocolate instead of coffee, let them go. If you can't tolerate their morning breath, let them go. If you don't like the way they talk and carry themselves, let them go. If you can't stand how loud and vocal they are about things, let them go. If their ideas and theories bother you, let them go. If you only choose the parts you want to love, it's unfair to continually keep them and stir their hearts.

If you can't love everything about them, don't hold them back. Don't keep them, because you're only hurting each other; you're trapping them in a dead-end relationship. If you find their flaws uncompromisable, let someone else love them.

Because someone will. For everything that they are and without asking them to change.

Someone out there will put up to every lame, miserable, and unacceptable character. Someone out there will listen to every secret and will respect every belief. Someone out there will stand the worst of days and will have the patience to understand. Someone out there at the end of each day will have the courage to tell them they love them still, no matter how horrible they are at times. Someone who is ready to love them exactly for who they are. Someone out there will appreciate their moments and never think they're repulsive. Someone out there will look at them and see magic—see that they're enough, not too much of this or that but perfect with all their edges. Someone who will acknowledge how much love they can offer and will never complain about it. Someone who will love them for who they genuinely are. No ifs, no buts. Someone who will take all those things you called flaws and call them perfection.

Someone—probably not you—so let them go and allow them to find that person.

5

Right Now

Right now is the time you start listening to yourself. The time you start looking for your own particular voice. Renouncing all the things people wanted you to become and all the things people wanted you to accomplish. Minimizing what they think is best for you and just paying attention to what truly mesmerizes your heart. Right now is the time you figure out your stance—what makes you unique, what makes you you. Right now is the time you take time off from everything they made you believe you are.

Right now is the time you make your life about you; what ignites your bones, what thrills your skin. Right now is the time you put yourself first, undaunted of other people, careless of their opinions.

Right now is the time you be exactly who you want to be.

6

When You're About To Give Up

I hope you don't give up on love. No matter how many times you get hurt or how many people enter your life with flowers and leave you with broken fragments of yourself all over your bedroom floor. No matter how much they ruin you and kill your fire—I hope you don't lose your spark and your huge heart that always hopes for love, that always believes that there is a genuine, real love out there and that there will be people who are willing to offer it to you. There will be people who are willing to hold your soul with loving-kindness and honesty. I hope you always persevere and are always reminded that there are gracious people out there who are willing to make up for all the times people have battered you and injured your spirit. That there are people out there who are willing to keep all the promises they made, who are willing to go out of their way to make you smile, who are willing to surprise you, who would do anything just to see you ecstatic, secured, and well. There will be people out there who will look at you with so much affection in their eyes that you will be magnified in their love, as well, their love will radiate and vibrate in every corner of your body. No matter how awful and difficult your past has been, there will certainly be someone out there for you who wouldn't even dare to give you a heartache, who would ask forgiveness when they need to, who will respect you and hold you as if they're holding the universe and they will hold accountability for it.

7

My Days Aren't Always The Same

Some days I don't understand people. Some days I do. Some days I see them walking out of my life and not caring about how I am or if I'm holding up well. Some days I receive messages that say they actually miss me. Some days I don't even notice their shadow and it's as if they don't need me in their life anymore. Some days they question what the hell is happening, but some days they just let everything slide, they let everything crash, they let everything break—and that's the confusing part. Why do we go through so much in our relationship with people? I mean, if we want them in our lives, why not make them stay? If we love them, why not tell them? I don't get why keeping people around is such a difficult task. When did it become so difficult to just make an effort to keep the people who are veritably important in our lives? When did it become such a heavy job to make someone feel like they're worth keeping? Because you know what? To be honest, I'm sick of having to watch people come in and out. If you want out, just get out. If you want in, then stay.

11

8

You're Not For Everyone

Understand that some people may not appreciate you. Your works may never be good enough for some company and your art may look ugly to some, but realize that it's okay. That doesn't make you any less of an artist or less of a person, for that matter. You are still the best—not for all, but for some—and that some are the only ones that matters. *You are not for everyone.*

Understand that who you are may never be enough for someone. Not everyone you meet will see galaxies in your eyes, adore your quirks, or find your flaws stunning. You will meet many lovers and not everyone will stay. Some will walk away because you're too loud and some will leave because you're too free. Some will take off because you're too soft. You will always be too much of something, and changing yourself to fit them is not the solution. You don't alter yourself. You remain you and you will find your person. You will find someone who would finally see galaxies in your eyes, who would look at you with clarity. And you'll find that person. For now, just remember *you are not for everyone.*

Understand that the reality of life is opportunity and talent. It doesn't matter how talented you are at something, if your opportunity never comes, then it's not for you. You just have to find what you're stunningly passionate about and try your hardest to seek your very own opportunity. *You're meant for something, but not for everything.*

Understand that some connections will cease because you will grow. You will have different desires and different interests and it's uncontrollable. You can't adjust your whole life just so you can keep a connection. Not all are forever; some are bound to end, some are bound

12

to live long. The best thing you could do is to find connections that grow with you through it all. Once you find that, you'll realize *you're not for everyone—and that's absolutely okay.*

9

When I Realize I Am What I Think

I stopped telling myself I'm lonely. I stopped telling myself I'm alone, that I'm a failure and that I'm good for nothing. I stood up and fought my own demons, those little voices who constantly wrestle in my head telling me things I don't want to hear, things that make me anxious, things that make my problem even tougher to overcome. I stopped letting the negativity control me and who I should be. I shut off all those voices and I started telling myself that I am capable; I can do whatever it is I put my mind into. I tell myself how strong my mind is and that if I say good things to myself, I might actually be doing myself a favor. I tell myself that I am what I think. So I convince myself over and over again that I am worth it, that I am whole and that I can survive. I can burn brighter. I can set the world on fire, put it out, and set it alight again—over and over again.

10

You Don't Have To Know

You don't have to know, you know. You don't have to be so obsessed about finding out what's in store for you, what's going to happen tomorrow or next month or next year, if you're on the right track, or if you're not going to regret the steps you take—NO. You don't have to be doing things to constantly control your future. You don't have to always be rushing, to always be drowning in worries and fears. Relax, slow down; you're driving yourself crazy. You won't figure your whole life in five days. Everything takes time; every single thing flourishes at its own pace. You breathe and you focus on the now. You rest your soul. You trust time. When you learn to just allow things to happen, they will blossom in the right season and you'll be surprised by just how splendid they are. Embrace the uncertainty; take big scary steps. Sometimes you don't have to know, you just have to trust your heart and go for it. You trust the voice inside you that believes in you. You don't have to know everything right now—you don't have to be frightened, as well—you just have to be excited and willing. You just have to go out there and ride the waves today. What's to come? Honey, it will be revealed in time.

11

People Do Not Ruin Labels, Labels Ruin People

How about we just ditch the labels and just be human? Human beings with hearts. Human beings with enough compassion, kindness, and generosity. Human beings who are more concerned about the things they do out of the tenderness of their hearts than the things they do out of the brackets they belong to. Human beings who realize that there's no point in fighting over who's better. Human beings who quit conversations that disrespect and judge one another and lead nowhere; who just push each other farther away instead of pulling one another closer. Human beings who actually treat each other with the same treatment they desire to attain. Human beings who meet halfway and descend from the pedestals they place themselves on. Human beings who live a life with equality, without condemnation and discrimination. Human being who live a life that celebrates all kind of differences with honesty and authentic love. Then maybe living would not be this complicated.

12

To The Unbelievers

The next time they go around thinking
they know you better than you do,
tell them you know what you want,
tell them you know where you're good at,
tell them you have passions; you have dreams,
tell them you know what you're made for,
and what you're made of.
Tell them you know better.

13

Perfect Love

There's a perfect love,
a love that won't abuse you,
a love that won't leave you devastated
but instead a love that will pick you up
when you are at your most broken
and does its best to restore you
and love you til you stop hurting
love you til you're good as new—
it's true. It exists. It's in Christ.

14

What You Don't Deserve

At 13, you don't deserve someone who calls you ugly or fat. You don't deserve to be surrounded by people who terrorize you and kill your confidence. You don't deserve someone who makes you believe you're not beautiful, that you need to try harder to be accepted.

At 16, you don't deserve to fall in love with someone who handles you with zero respect. You don't deserve someone who calls you a slut and makes you feel low about yourself. You don't deserve someone who sees you as a 2 AM habit. You don't deserve someone who steadily lectures you about how you dress, how you talk, how you are entirely. You don't deserve someone who physically and verbally abuses you just because they think they own you.

At 19, you don't deserve friendships that discourage you. People who invariably and repeatedly ravage your dreams. You don't deserve someone who makes you conclude that you can't do it, that you will not cut it. You don't deserve someone who never drives you to pursue neither your tiny whim nor your massive plans.

At 23, you don't deserve a dictator. You don't deserve someone who controls your choices and decisions. You don't deserve someone who tries to live your life for you. You don't deserve someone who views you like you're a work of their own hands, like it's their job to shape you into their monumental idea of who you should be. You don't deserve someone who meticulously molds you to fit them. You don't deserve someone who mocks your soul, who does not take into consideration your singularity.

Because really, you don't deserve to be tamed. You deserve to go out there and live your life without worry, without fear. You deserve to light up and set the world on fire with your wit, courage, and kindness.

And for the rest of your life, you deserve to do exactly just that.

15

Even For A Day

You can ease your mind, you know.

You can enjoy the morning breeze and sip your coffee without thinking about what you'll do next.

You can cast out your worries and doubts; you can try to shut down your anxieties and turn off your insecurities. You can breathe and take things slowly, even just for a day.

You can stop pressuring yourself; you can stop pleasing people. You can brave rejections and regrets. You can do things that might not benefit you now; you can move outside your comfort zone. You can stop looking out for yourself. You can live unsecured and uncertain even just for a day.

You can give and take, you can live with regard to other human beings, you can carry their burdens instead of always dwelling on your own personal battles.

You can wake up today with a smile on your face and carefree. You can think about this very moment and delight in it. You can bask in the now. You can drown in joy. You can sing louder, kiss sweeter, and love deeper.

You can just live, you know. Even just for a day.

16

Love

I learned to love—to *really* love—when I realized that the world does not revolve around me. It does not orbit around my wants or needs. I learned to love when I realized that loving is more about the people we love, not ourselves. That sometimes it's not all about the love we deserve but the love *they* deserve and the love we should give. That it's okay to adjust at times, to go a little out of our usual habits to make them smile and make them feel worth it. That it's okay to put their needs above ours; that it's okay to be a little selfless at times as much as it's okay to be selfish.

I learned to love when I realized that love isn't me, it's the people around me. And if we throw love around like confetti, living will be a lot easier.

17

I Want People To See Me

I want people to see me. Not the anxiously edited version of me, no. I mean the bare, honest me. In the most striving, disoriented, staggering, flawed form. The version who wakes up apathetic some mornings, who goes to work with hair tied up and wearing the usual white sneakers. The version without an ample amount of make-up to cover all the cracks, without plenty of smile to hide all the weak spots. The version who can't even pull herself together at times. The version who has no idea as to what she'll do, where she'll go. The version who's too attached and needy with the people she recklessly loves. The version who fears the future and fears death. The version who's ultimately vulnerable; the version who doesn't even have enough weapons to slay her own dragons.

I want people to see me like this. Without lies and pretensions. Without filters and nice captions. I want people to see me—the same version I see every morning when I look at the mirror.

Because for what it's worth, she gives me one more reason to go on, despite it all.

Despite it all.

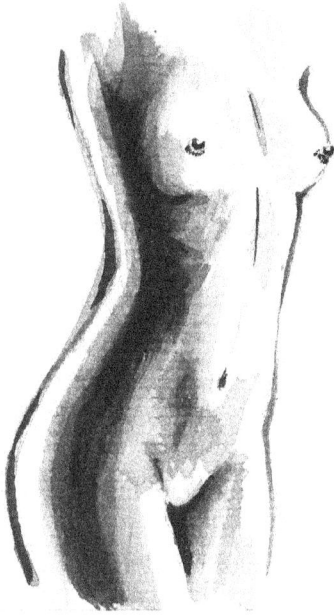

Maybe It's Time

Maybe it's time you stop allowing tomorrow to take too much of today. The time you stop worrying about what might happen tomorrow, time you stop saturating yourself with worries about next month or what you have to attain within your lifetime. Maybe you need to take a step back and just center on today. Ask yourself what makes you happy today. What makes you fulfilled today? What makes your life worth living and dying for, today?

Maybe it's time you quit forcing yourself to be sufficient for the rest of life and allow yourself to just be sufficient today. Maybe it's time you release yourself from your five-year plan and just be someone you'll be proud of today.

Maybe it's time you drop thinking about living but actually live.

Meaning

I've always wonder how to live my life right.
You know, how do I look back and say *I did it right*
What if there's no way to do it right?
What if the core of living is not actually doing things right
but just finding meaning in every single thing I do?
In every aspect of who I am?
I hope I get to do that,
before it's too late.

20

Ambitions

One major lesson you learn as you mature in life is that you really don't have to listen to what the world tells you. You don't have to turn on the opinions of other people. You honestly don't need their validation on literally anything and most definitely not on your passion, not on your art. You do what you love. Don't care what they think. Don't care what they say. For as long as you believe in yourself, nothing really matters more. You are a work of art in progress. Surround yourself with people who believe in you, who do not belittle what you do, and who absolutely see you as a star that shines as vividly as it can in the darkest of nights. Trust me when I say that you are bound to do incredible things, and really, darling, you don't need to wait for people's green lights nor their theories. What you need are insights, and you can only get that from the ones who permit you to fly. So go create your art and create it with madness and passion. Soar higher than ever before. I'm with you.

21

I Hope You See Yourself The Way I See You

I hope you see your eyes in such a way that I see it—full of life and love and desire to love those around you. I hope you see your heart the way I see it, so gentle, so true, and so wide. I hope you see your mind the way I see it, overflowing with riveting ideas.

I hope you see yourself the way I see you. Then you would see a captivating human being, living-breathing proof that people can be warm and gracious. I hope you see yourself the way I see you; then maybe you would see how capable you are. How substantial and astonishing you are, then maybe you would believe in yourself more. I hope you reach the depths of your soul, then maybe you would love yourself more.

22

Feel

When we lose the part of ourselves that is open, the part that is hurting and the part that is celebrating—we lose the most startling part about being a human. We lose the possibility to make irreplaceable connections; we lose the most breathtaking part of ourselves—feeling. So feel. Feel the disappointment, feel the love, feel the forgiveness, and feel it all deeply.

23

To Women

The next time they tell you—
Don't wear that, or
that is too short, or
you're asking for it, or
you should be expecting that, or
you're not even aware of your body.

Tell them—
"This my body, I can wear whatever I want
and you need to understand that I'm not asking for it.
This is my body; I own it.
The only thing you own is your manners,
and it's not my problem
you don't know a thing about respect
nor your lack of self-control."

Then continue to speak with conviction:
"Stop teaching women to cover up.
Instead, start educating our society that rape is not acceptable
and women are not sexual objects."

Because we're not. We're not.

24

He Doesn't Own You

His job is not to alter you, not to tell you you're showing too much skin or that what you're wearing makes you obscene. It is not noticing what lipstick you have on and telling you you look hideous. It's not his task to lecture you about your size or your legs or your hair ,for that matter. His job is to love it all, and if he can't do that, he better go. Because this is your body, this is your sanctuary; you can do whatever you want, wear whatever you want, and he has no right to *anything*. He's just a visitor.

Stop Waiting For Your Entire Life To Unfold

Stop being terrified, stop being so consumed by fear, of the ambiguities along the way. Stop walking away from the things you love and the people you care for. Stop anticipating a green light for your life to begin so you could finally go to places and do the things you always wanted to try. Stop begging people to stay, and stop holding on to those who cannot carry your big heart. Stop finding satisfaction in other people's passion and achievements. Stop riding on someone else's faith, stop depending your happiness on how people warily pictured it. Stop crying in the rain because you can't see your own sunshine. Stop disappointing yourself by tolerating what you know you definitely hate.

Stop living life like you're on a cliff, like you're too timid to push beyond the walls and move a little bigger because you might stumble those around you. Stop apologizing for every decision, for every choice.

Just stop.

26

You Are Enough

It sounds cliché. Like a broken disc on repeat, like your worn out sneakers, like 37th street—all too familiar. But it's the ultimate truth you keep on forgetting.

You are enough. Believe it.

Your freckles, your legs and your eyes—they're perfect. You are worth all the odds and all the hardships. You are worth all the affection and devotion your huge heart can give. You are worth all the appreciation your tiny body can exhale. You are worth loving, every single minute of your life.

So go be your own first love. Fall in love with yourself and stay passionately in love.

27

You Have Nothing To Prove

You don't have to prove how right you are for choosing that person. You are only human and you only love. There's strength and audacity in that; not everyone can love like you do. Never, ever apologize for loving people and for not making labels a greater deal than your heart.

28

Finding Fulfillment

May we stop finding fulfillment in materials things, in the number of zeros in our bank account or the model of our car. May we find fulfillment in the things that are not tangible, in the things we cannot see, touch, or hear but just feel. May we stop finding fulfillment in recognition, in pride, in achievements. May we find fulfillment in how we honor other people, how we serve them, and how we love them. May we stop finding fulfillment in personal things, in accumulating as much as we can for our own benefits and consumption. May we find fulfillment in how we leave our fingerprints on the lives of the people we meet, how we move, encourage, and inspire their lives. May we find fulfillment in how we show generosity and goodness. May we just find fulfillment in how we walk with people, how we contribute to their being, and how we push them to be who they are meant to be.

May we find the fullness of fulfillment in the smallest of things that we do for people. Not for ourselves. Because really, the world is too selfish already.

29

Being Human

We aren't always pretty. We aren't always alluring. Neither is life. Sometimes there won't be enough filters to make something more enticing than the reality of it. Sometimes we can't conceal all our flaws and blemishes. Sometimes there won't be a right angle to hide all the unseemly and undesirable parts. Sometimes we just have to accept ourselves thoroughly, together with our own process, our own conflicting situations and breakthroughs. Sometimes we just have to realize that we all have distinct encounters, a series of wins and losses, detours and failures, filth and tragedies. Sometimes we just have to embrace all the parts we hate as much as the parts we adore for these are the things that make us genuine, things that make us wonderfully one of a kind and authentic, these are all the things that make us human, very human.

All The Ugly Parts

They tell you they love you when it's easy, when the scene is breath-taking, and the night glistens and the stars dance. They will tell you they love when you're kind, when you're patient and understanding. They will tell you they love you when you're smiling and your heart is beaming. They will tell you they love when your lips are full of stories as exciting as it is when kissing you. They will tell you they love you when you're too attached. They will tell you they love you when your eyes are shining and it's a good day.

They will tell you they love you when it's a good day. When all is well, when all is right. Just how they wanted it. They will tell you they love you when it's easy sailing, when it's favorable. They will tell you they love you when you're someone they can manipulate you to be who they want, when you're strong, but not too strong. Not when you're ugly and messy, not when you're in a bad mood. No.

They won't tell you they love when you're difficult to handle. When you're being a pain in the ass, when you're too much of a woman. They won't tell you they love you when it's impossible to deal with you, when you're too annoying, messy, problematic, anxious, needy, clingy, and rough.

They won't tell you they love you because they don't. Because if they did love you, they would love all the ugly parts first.

31

Beautiful People

People love to love beautiful, shiny people—those who are enchanting and lovely to look at. Those who are amazing to hold and extravagant to own. But how about the ugly ones, the ones with bruises and damages, the ones with a past, issues, and problems. How about the works in progress, the scarred; how about the ones bleeding?

What happens to them when everyone else is too busy loving the beautiful ones?

On Social Media

When I think about where I spent most of my time, I would see myself disgusted. I'm appalled with how I begin the day, how I finish the day, and how I make the most of the in betweens. I'm sickened about how involved I am in other people's lives. How I stalk them to death 24/7, how I scroll through Facebook like a maniac, how I manage my way through Instagram measuring my life to theirs. It's exasperating how I allow these sites to trigger jealousy, comparison, envy, and even depression. It's infuriating how I drive myself even crazier.

On top of it all, the only thing I'm doing is destroying myself one social media site at a time, in my own time, with my own effort.

We need to stop doing this to ourselves. We need to realize how thin and soft our skins are and how fragile our hearts are; we need to start taking good care of them. Releasing ourselves from all the toxicity of this world, washing away every single thing that made us feel bad about who we are. Away from the things the poison our being, time and time again. And just breathe fresher and fresher air until we're feeling good, until we're better.

33

Victorious

There's a beauty when we struggle. When we're in the midst of chaos, when we're honest that we can't do it, that we can't fight on our own, because only then will we seek help. And when we whisper the name of Jesus, when we lift our hands to heaven and ask for it to come and help us through—He will. He will always bring us our victory. He will always render us triumphant.

34

Stop

Stop going after people who only love you when it's convenient for them, when it's easy. Stop handing yourself to people who only love you when you're beautiful, when you're well-rounded. Because really, they don't know the meaning of the word love. They only know the meaning of the word sad.

35

We All Want To Be Okay

Because being okay is enough. But you know you can be more than okay, more than settling for what's right there—you can be beyond that. You can be fantastic. You can be amused. You can be ecstatic. You can be marvelous. You can aim for more than just okay because for what it's worth, you deserve to be beyond okay.

When I Was Younger

When I was younger, I always wondered what it was like to be somebody else, what it was like to walk in somebody else's shoes. To wake up in somebody else's house, with somebody else's mother dealing with somebody else's siblings. To experience somebody else's emotion, to endure their day-to-day strife and how they measure to get over their own endeavors—all because I was always amazed at how people overcome. How they soar higher than their circumstances, how they dance in their situations, how they fix themselves with the silver linings, how they are transformed magnificently by their trials. I wanted to carry their spirit, adopt their strength, and channel their bravery. That's all.

Until it became hostile. I wanted to walk in somebody else's shoes not because of compassion or empathy anymore but simply because I wanted to be them, and I lost myself in the process.

It's ironic how I long to be somebody else every single day but never myself.

37

I'm Fine

Saying "I'm fine" becomes tiresome. It becomes a substance that con-
taminates you cell by cell. It corrupts your dreams and gets you stuck.
It drowns you in a sea of comfort and ease. And that harms you; that
murders the light inside you. So, I urge you to stop saying you're fine.
Stop saying your job is fine if it's terrible. Stop saying your lover is
fine if they're not inspiring you every morning, if they're not good for
you, if they're dull. Stop saying you're fine when you're really not fine.

Allow honesty to emanate out of your heart, and trust me, you cannot imagine the bliss that comes from that. Once you start being
honest with yourself, with what you really feel, what you really long
for, you can be free in such a level that you'll find your place, you'll
find your stance. And before you know it, one day you will wake up
and you're not just faking it. You're glowing and joy is beaming out of
you, and you realize you're not just fine, you're magical.

What I Will Teach My Children

At the end of it all, I will not teach my children to be pretty. I will not teach them to always be presentable, to always make sure their eyebrows are on point. I will not teach them to eat less and less to become thinner. I will not teach them to be perfect in all their ways, to always be confident in the newest name-brand bag, in their career title, in other material things. I will not teach them to buy the latest gadget and always be on track with the trend. I will not teach them to accumulate as much wealth as they can. I will not teach them to work for the money, for their ego and pride. I will not teach them to choose the picture-perfect man or woman and marry them. I will not teach them to think they're better than anyone, to condemn other people, or judge people just because they're not the same in some ways. I will not teach them to be the smartest ass in the room. I will not teach them to go to workshops and find talents and be a shining star. I will not teach them to be an architect or an engineer because people will think highly of them. I will not teach them to always be the strongest one, the one who never had a tear in their eyes.

As much as I can, I will teach them to be human.

To accept the fact that they are flawed in many ways. I will teach them that there will surely be bad hair days, acne moments, and fat lazy months. I will teach them that they are nowhere near perfect but that doesn't make them any less beautiful. I will teach them that it's their imperfections that makes them uniquely stunning. I will teach them that sizes are irrelevant. They can be healthy and not a size 0. I will teach them to embrace failures; I will always remind them that their skills and abilities will not always fit the company they're applying to and that's okay, that doesn't make them any less worth it for the job. They're deserving of other jobs, other companies—maybe brighter and bigger ones. I will teach them that dream companies exist as long as they love what they do, as long as they're passionate about their craft, that sometimes dream companies doesn't pay them as much as they have expected. I will teach them that true confidence does not lie in the big things, in the obvious and recognizable milestones, but it flickers in the littlest of things we do. It's finishing homework, going out without contour, and standing up for what you believe in and upholding what you don't. I will teach them to marry someone they ultimately love, someone who is affectionate to their soul and does not sabotage their magic, regardless of their bank account or religion. I will teach them to collect memories, to travel more, to buy experiences instead of tangible things. I will teach them to acquire generosity more. I will teach them to do good works from the bottom of their heart with nothing but clean intentions.

Above all else, I will teach them to be compassionate, to be there for other people when they need them, to be present, to listen, to bring encouragement, and to motivate. I will teach them to know humility, to accept opinions and honor other views. I will teach them bravery in weakness, strength in tears, fortitude in healing. And lastly, I will teach them to love; love God with everything and love people without discrimination. I will teach them to always be kind because a life well lived is a life filled with nothing but kindness and love.

39

Background Noise

At the end of the day, what matters most is how it makes you feel, how it contributes to your way of life, how it creates in you a better individual, how it encourages you to be kind and to live a life well-lived, a life overflowing with gratefulness and joy. How all of your choices forge your heart, how it handmade you to be someone that not only you will be proud of but also that voice inside you. That's the only thing that matters. Everything else is background noise.

Part 2

The Storm

40

Loving and Losing

Love them as beautifully as you can,
Kiss them as passionately as you can,
Hold them as tightly as you can,

Because one day,
they will hold your face
and it will feel a lot like goodbye,

Because it is.

And the next morning you'll wake up
with nothing but scars and memories
reminding you of what it was like kissing them,
being next to them,
loving them
and then losing them.

41

He

He came like he needs no permission, like he can just sweep me off my feet, and make me fall hard in love, and kiss me so gently, hold me so tightly, like it's his calling. And then he fled, swiftly as a hurricane, ruining everything he touched—and at that very second, I forgot how healing works.

42

Disaster

It's when you find someone
who loves you with kindness in their eyes
gentleness in their hands
respect in their lips
comfort in their shoulders
safety in their chest
and you let them walk away
just because you refuse to run.

43

How Tragedy Happens

Tragedy happens when we think we can never lose someone,
when we take them for granted,
when we stop appreciating,
stop lending an ear,
and stop reaching out with loving hands.

Tragedy happens when we become too confident
that they'll never let go,
because they can't

but they can,
and eventually
they will.

And the tragedy goes on
when we don't make an effort to keep them,
when we let the problem be bigger than the solution,
when we let pride be louder than the relationship,
when we allow them to go
instead of making them stay.

How You Destroy Her

You destroy her the moment she stops being an adventure. When she's no longer exciting, when rolling over to see her in the morning doesn't lead to butterflies anymore, and when kissing her has become a task. You destroy her when you let the fire die, when you let the spark cease. When taking her out to places doesn't stun you anymore, when you'd rather hang out with people other than her, when seeing her smile is not an advantage anymore.

You destroy her when you no longer appreciate her, when she doesn't bring happiness and sunshine anymore. You destroy her when you look at her and all you see is lack, when she has become a burden rather than a gift. When being with her every day has become hard work and it's easier to just shout at her to end an argument rather than patiently explain what's wrong, when you'd rather walk away than make everything better, when you'd rather shut the door instead of opening up and letting her in.

You destroy her when she's no longer an inspiration but an obligation. When everything you do for her feels like a drag, when it's no longer convenient for you to bring her flowers or take her out to a simple dinner. You destroy her when her words don't inspire you to be a better person, when you feel like she's no longer contributing to who you aspire to be considering that she once encouraged you to dream higher and made you believe that you can be the best, that you can be whoever you long to be, that you have the talent and the confidence to be such.

You destroy her when you no longer see her for her depth, when all you see is a single star that was once an entire universe, when you only see a river that was once an ocean.

You destroy her when you tell her you love her but you let her go to bed doubting if days will ever be like they were before, when you allow her to sleep uncertain of whether or not you still feel the same passion for her and with pain wondering if she is lacking in some point, if there's anything she could've done differently that may change your heart. You destroy her when you steal her joy.

You destroy her when it no longer hurts you when you're hurting her. When you're damaging her and wrecking her but it no longer stings. When 'sorry' doesn't matter more than your ego and pride.

You destroy her when you destroy her light, when you no longer see beauty in her eyes but a catastrophe. When all the reasons why you chose her and loved her so right have become the reasons why you destroyed her, when you lost track of all the reasons why she caught your eye, why you found her spirit striking, why you found a home in her heart, why you wanted her, why you loved her. And you let her go because letting go is easier than reminding yourself all the 'why's you already forgot.

And that's exactly how you destroy her.

45

Father

They say when you love someone, everything about them is breath-takingly beautiful at first. The first glance, the first touch, the first word—it's like nothing is ever unlikable. Everything is pleasant and alluring. It's like you cannot see or find anything you don't like; it's like everything about them is worth all the love in the world.

But they also say that it's only in the beginning, that as time passes by, you'll find all the wrongs, the things you hate, the habits you dislike, and the love will cease.

I don't believe it. Because from the very first day I saw you, I knew I would love you. And I loved you deeply. As deep as the oceans and as wide as the skies, I loved you. You became my favorite and I am not exaggerating. And even though 22 years have passed us by just like that, I would still look at you and I would still feel the same love.

I loved you all the same.

Years have passed and I still cannot see anything wrong or anything I don't like. And it doesn't matter if another 22 years pass, I know...I will love you all the same.

Always
and maybe forever.

Leaving

Don't ever mistake their leaving as your shortcoming. Don't blame yourself if they didn't commit longer, or if they decided to let go. It's really not you. There isn't anything you could've done differently that would have made them stay. There isn't anything you can change that would make them love you a year more. It's not because of how devoted you are to them; it's not because you loved them too much.

You should know that you loved them just right.

Your heart is too wide, too vast, and too loving, and that's not your fault. It's not your fault they can't handle your heart. It's not your fault that they can't swim in its depth. It's also not your fault for giving it away to people who fumble its weight, who think it's too heavy, who can't take care of it with utter responsibility and gentleness.

And above all, know also that this heart is yours.
Please hold it, guard it, and love it even when no one can—
especially when no one can.

47

The Greater Fear

I fear the day you'll realize you don't want to be with me anymore,
the day you'll realize I no longer excite you
and there's nothing else I can do to make the situation good.

I fear the day you'll lose interest and you would want to move forward without me.
I fear the day you'll say your goodbye
and walk out of my door then out of my life.
I fear the day you'll come to the idea that I'm no longer worth it,
not worth your time, effort, and energy.

I fear the day you'll just leave,
the day you'll just stop.

Because nothing hurts more than proving the fact that not all love is permanent,
that it can end,
and forget
all the reasons why it even started.

Dirtiest

Loving gets hard sometimes. No matter how hard you love there will always be rejection, offenses, hatred, and frailties. There will always be situations that will provoke unwanted feelings, unsought for actions. Loving is never perfect. To be honest, I don't know how to love anyone perfectly. I always disappoint the people I love. I break their hearts. I do things that make them angry and trigger them to leave. Sometimes I even say I love them but do otherwise. I don't commit to my promises; I let them down. I'm not there when they need me. I let them bask in a pool of loneliness, anxiety, and depression. I let them drown in hopelessness, saturated in uncertainty and fear. I lack. I always lack.

And no human being has ever loved me perfectly. I have encountered every kind of setback from every single person who swore they loved me. I have had my heart broken by every single person who swore that the thing they hated the most is to see me destroyed. I have cried over people who swore they would not be able to forgive themselves if they ever caused me pain.

We lack. We always lack.

So just when I thought I'll never experience a love so perfect, without any flaw—He looked at me and carried me home. He embraced me with forgiveness and held me tightly with gentleness and goodness. He loved me like I deserve His unconditional love, like I don't know sin, like everything I do pleased Him, like I never did anything shameful in my whole life. He wanted me in a way no one ever wanted me before. *He chose me like I'm the best there is.* I'm not deserving, but still He loved me without any shade of fear, hopelessness, disappointment, or sorrow.

He was the purest giver of love and I was the dirtiest recipient.

49

I Wonder What You Think Of Me Now

I wonder if you would look at me
and still feel the same unconditional love.
I wonder if you would tell stories about me now
with so much enthusiasm
still.

I wonder if you would encourage me to go on down this path
or you would shake your head in disappointment.
I wonder if you're smiling
whenever you would see what became of me
or you'll think to yourself, *maybe if I raised her better...*

I do hope I'm making you proud,
of all my becoming,
of all my mess,
of all my pieces scattered everywhere.

I hope you see how hard I'm trying,
putting my life together,
now that you're gone.

All The 'Why's

I don't know why they left you. I don't know what triggered them to walk away. Maybe it's the gentleness in your hands or the authenticity in your eyes. I don't know why they thought you're not for them. Maybe it's because you love with so much passion or maybe because you care too much. I don't know the reasons why they thought it wouldn't work out. Maybe it's your infinite kindness or your unfailing respect.

I don't know.

But I do know why timing and opportunity allowed them to get out of your door and way out of your life, and it's because someone's coming. Someone will walk into your life and will desire nothing more but the gentleness in your hands and the authenticity in your eyes. Someone will fight hard just to experience your passionate love and deep-seated care. Someone will pursue you just so they can roll over in bed every single morning to see your infinite kindness and unfailing respect.

And that someone wouldn't trade you, not even for the world.

51

I Don't Remember His Scent Anymore

And that will always be a reminder that he's gone. Gone. I'll never be able to calm myself around the safest corners of his arms. Gone. I'll never be able to feel his warmth ever again. Gone. I'll never get to express how much he means to me. Gone. All the pieces of every feeling, every experience we shared is now just a memory gradually fading into thin air.

The Ugly Truth About Losing You

Honesty finds me today.

I realize there was no point in lying to myself or to people. There was no point in pretending that I was okay, that I know what I'm doing, that I am doing well when it comes to pulling myself together.

Because the ugly truth is, I cry whenever I remember you. My heart throbs whenever I see your favorite shirt. My legs grow weak whenever I lay in your bed. I can still feel your warmth. And I can see myself scattered everywhere; I can't go on. I am falling apart from relationships, from passions, and even from myself. I don't know what I'm supposed to do with my life. I lost all sense of direction, motivation, and purpose. I know you're not proud of what I am becoming right now, but know that I did not regret building my life upon you. No.

I just hope I find the strength to dream again, to just rise above all this. Maybe there's truth when they say that grief doesn't change you, it reveals you.

And this might be who I am, father.

53

If You Stayed A Little Longer

I would've known what to do, I would've had solid plans to push through. I would've not been this disoriented, baffled kid who has no idea what she really wants to do, what she *has* to do. Maybe if you stayed a little while longer, I would've not lost my mind, my inspiration, or my motivation. Maybe if you were still here, I would know exactly my devotion, my aim, my inclination, and I wouldn't be looking for my very own purpose in all the wrong places.

If you were still here, maybe my life wouldn't be this big trainwreck; maybe I would be doing just fine.

54

Wounded Souls and Broken Hearts

People need to realize that there's nothing wrong with wounded souls and broken hearts. Life is never perfect and you're just killing yourself trying to be.

55

How I Remember You

The thing about losing a loved one is that once they're gone, every single memory you have will come vividly back like it just happened five minutes ago.

I remembered everything. *Every single memory.*

I remember all the sweet hugs, the genuine kisses, the fulfilling 'I love you's, the dates, the adventures, the meaningful walks and talks, the times I would gladly bring him to the airport, the goodbyes, the one year waiting period till he was home again, the non-stop phone calls, the unlimited 'how are you?'s, the cute packages, the thoughtful gifts, the stories, the excuses so I wouldn't get in trouble. I remember that one time he rushed me to the hospital because I burned myself, that moment he panicked because I was bleeding, how he was always mad at me during those days I was too lazy to take a bath and I didn't want to clean up my mess, the times he'd bring me to school and pick me up from places.

I remember the sacrifices, the tears, the years spent away so he could give us better lives and a better future. The work he endured so we could enjoy, the suffering and the pain so we could live conveniently. The times he thought of us first before he thought of himself. The times he was such an amazing, kind-hearted, patient man. The times his plans were revolving around his family, what's best for us, and how he could do things for us.

I remembered it all.

I remember the first time we rushed him to the hospital and how my world came crashing down into a million tiny pieces. How scared I was—terrified. How terrified I was just thinking about the fact that I might lose him anytime, how I don't want to live more than half of my life without him. I remember how he would want to see me and listen to me instead of the doctors. I remember how he overcame, how he survived.

But I also remember the second time we rushed him to the same hospital (which I swear I hate). I remember how strong he was then, how he fought, how he didn't want to leave us. I remember how selfless he was in everything, that even in his most vulnerable phase he still thought of me and of his family. I remember how he held my hand and didn't want me to leave his side. I remember how he loved me in perfect detail, in such a genuine way.

I remember the good old days, the moments together. How he would always be the first person I want to tell all the good news, how he was the person I loved the MOST in the entire universe without exaggeration. How he would always be the first person I wanted to share my success at school or anything with. I remember how I would tell people all of his good traits and they would see how much he means to me. He meant the world to me. I remember why I am motivated, why I do what I do, why I strive hard in life and it's all because I want to give him a comfortable life in return.

I remember all the life lessons, from the simplest ones like 'be nice to any waitress', to being generous to a homeless man. How I should value my education, how I should work tremendously hard if I wanted something. How important it is to just forgive people and not hold any grudge against them. I remember how I should chase after my dreams and what I really want in life more than I pursue any man. How I should love my family and the people that are really close to me. How I should take good care of them so I wouldn't lose them, how I should be compassionate and loving.

I remember how his heart is as wide as the skies. How his soul is as bright as million stars combined. I remember how he was very resilient in fighting, how courageous he was overcoming all the waves the ocean threw. I remember how generous he was in giving not just to his family but to anyone who needs it, how he was always giving people the chance and the opportunity they need. How he strongly believe that there is good karma, that what goes around comes around, how he was always kind and loving. I remember how soft he was, how caring and sacrificial. I remember him as a strong man, a man of his word.

And I will also remember how it hurts to know that he is gone and I just had a sweet, incredible 22 years with him. I want more; I want more years, more days, more moments and more memories. I will remember the ache and the sorrow of losing someone like him. I will remember how this is better for him because I know he is in a better place. That the pain and the suffering are over, the burden is gone. I'm joyful that it will be easier for him, that he can now sleep well without any hint of pain. No more aches, no more sorrow, only gladness and peace. I will remember how he made me the happiest daughter in the world knowing he is no longer in pain and how I am also the saddest one knowing he will never come back.

I will remember how he will miss out on more than half of my life, how I will grow, how I will evolve, how I will fall in love, how I will get marry some day or maybe start a business, cry over a lost someone, a failed pitch. How he will miss out on all our future plans that he promised would wait until pushed through. How he will miss the future nights I will cry myself to sleep, I will fight, I will fall down, I will get up and I will survive life. I will remember how he tried—tried to not miss out on all of this, and even though he failed at trying, he did not fail as a father.

But above all, the thing that I will remember most is love, love brewed perfectly with pain.

The kind of pain I would love to endure an entire lifetime with, the kind of pain that I will remember and be glad, the kind that I will be reminded of why I work so hard today, why I am the way that I am today. The kind of pain that is altogether breathtaking and beautiful. The kind of pain that is forever engraved within the depths of my bones.

I will remember him, everywhere I look, everywhere I go, all our memories, all our experiences, and I know that half of who I am, half of my soul will always be a reminder of him.

He was a great father. And I will forever be grateful I had him. I wouldn't have it any other way.

Be assured I can make it through. Because for what it's worth, you raised me well. You raised a strong woman.

I'll be okay.

56

Terrifying

The most terrifying part about falling in love
is not the exact moment they leave,
not the moment it ends.

It's actually the following days, the months, and the years.
It's the process of breaking every single day
like it's the very first time you ever break,
it's the devastation and the frustration,
it's the begging and the self-pity,
it's the 'why?'s and the 'how?'s and the 'what could I do?'
it's the hope, the expectations, the 'oh, please come back!'
it's the pieces that are too destroyed to even be put back together,
it's the constant shaking, cracking
and undeniably no sign of mending.

And what's more terrifying is
encountering love again and then walking away from it,
not because you're too scared
but because you're too scarred.

57

Tomorrow

I hope when I encounter your name tomorrow, the thing that I will remember is our first touch and how tender your hand was, our first glance and how earnest your eyes were, our first kiss and how delicate and heartfelt it was.

I hope I will remember how you mastered each quirk, how you wrapped your mind around every idea, how you recalled every tiny but essential detail. I hope I will remember your substantial confessions, your unwavering desires, your brave love. I hope I just remember all the loving and the mending, the caring and the holding, the longing and the forgiving.

Not the arguments and the judgments. Not the lies and the sins. Not the burns and the cuts. Not the trauma and the bruises. Not the yelling and the hurting, not the heavy breathing and the gasping, not the crying and the collapsing. Not the door shutting and the hearts shattering. Not the ravaging and the exploding.

Not that, I hope. Not that.

The Last Time

When was the last time you looked at her? The last time your attention was definitely penetrating through every deep-seated compo-
nent of her soul? When was the last time you weren't rushing but just
absorbing every detail, every color of her? When was the last time
you kissed her with your eyes closed and just floated through the
sensation, inhaling the closeness, the taste, the scent, the affection?
When was the last time you actually heard her with your heart open,
listening to every adoration, every yearning, every involvement?
When was the last time you told her you love her and unquestionably
held truth in it?

Because she's waiting for that.
Tangled in hope,
dragged by desperation,
and held down by loneliness,
she's still waiting.

59

Regrets

"Be with someone who looks at you like you're the most beautiful thing they had ever seen," she said.

And I thought, for the first years of being with her, I would always look at her smile and I know I have the most beautiful woman in the world.

I'm in love with her mind, with her words, and with her heart. She's independent, strong, and resilient. She can take care of herself and others. Her heart was so broad it could love a million people all at once. She's determined and bold. She's inspiring, not just to me but to almost everyone who encounters her. She is magical.

Until she wasn't.

Not anymore. After some time in the relationship, I looked at her and I didn't see beauty anywhere. I didn't feel lucky or blessed having her. With all truth, I saw disappointment, I saw weakness. I saw a scared, insecure, anxious, and sad little girl.

Perhaps I made her that way, or not. I don't know; what I do know is—*I'm no longer in love with her.*

So I let her go.

Now someone's holding her. With more love than I ever thought was possible. Someone's looking at her with full affection and attention, someone's listening to her and hearing every word, eager for every inspiration, every motivation. Someone's looking at her boldness and her bravery and her heart and actually admiring every single trait.

Someone's looking at her and is blessed to have her. Someone's holding her heart—this time with responsibility, this time with gentleness, this time with respect, and *this time with determination to actually keep it.*

I genuinely wish they wouldn't just so I could have her back.

60

Photographs

I don't want to see your photos anymore. I don't want to see your face. Not because I love you less now or because I hate you, or because of whatever bad reason you might think of.

I don't want to see your photos because I don't want to relive the ache. I don't want the pain that comes with seeing your smile, your tattoos, and your beautiful face. I don't want the longing that is intolerable and the heartache that is inexplicable.

I don't want all the dreadful things to play over and over again in my mind whenever I would see your face—our faces—that glowed with laughter as if we owned the world. I don't want to see how enthusiastic we were about our plans, how convinced and tenacious we were as if the world was fair and gentle, as if the world would always be on our side.

I don't want the infinity in our eyes like we owned forever, as if the joy won't end, as if we'll never part, as if no horrible thing awaits us.

I don't want the certainty and the dreams and the hopes that lives in our being as if everything would fall into place, as if life would always be sunshine and rainbows, as if the storm would never come to get us, as if there won't be any catastrophe somewhere down the road, as if things would only get better with time, as if you would always hold me when the night gets one shade darker and life becomes a little tougher.

I don't want to see the genuine future in our hearts, as if you would always stay, as if I would never lay awake in my bedroom crying myself to sleep and missing the hell out of you, as if you would always be there, as if you would never leave. As if.

Rusty Old Bookstore

And if I get another chance,
another shot to make things right
and go back to the very first moment
I met you—

when you were walking down 37th Street
towards that rusty old bookstore,
my eyes following your every step
and your lips smiling as our eyes finally met,
and, oh God, trust me I have never seen such beauty before;
I have never seen anything as real as you,

and as you gazed around each shelf
you picked up that book—
I knew I should smile back
but I didn't.
When I passed through
you whispered, *What do you think about the ending?*
I finally smiled back
and stopped by that corner of the rusty old bookstore,
as I watched how the entire trajectory of my life shifted,
in ways I never thought was possible—

So if I can go back
to that very moment,
that very second I saw you,
about to walk into that rusty old bookstore,
I swear,
Darling, I swear,

I would pass by
and I wouldn't look back.

62

If I See Her Again

If I see her again, I would tell her I'm sorry for that one particular night I let her sleep unsure of who she is in my life and how much of my heart she's really holding.

And then I'm going to say sorry for the following nights after that, the nights I let her sleep over and over again speculating if she's still important, if she's still enough or if I still love her all the same. I'm going to say sorry for the days that follow, the days she felt empty and ruined, feeling like I don't want to take care of her, of our relationship.

I'm going to apologize for the permanent wreckage; for taking things for granted, for taking her for granted.

I'm going to apologize for not acknowledging her light and her energy. I'm going to apologize for all the times I made her feel insufficient, for all the instances I didn't care, occasions I didn't exert any effort on fixing our misunderstandings, our petty arguments that turned into monstrous fights. I'm going to apologize for the holes I left, and for filling it with doubt and pain afterwards.

I'm going to tell her how sorry I really am, how I know how her worth, how I miss her, how I couldn't drape myself around the fact that I lost her, and how I want her back, so bad.

63

Until I'm Happy

"Until when will you love me?" I asked.

"What do you want to hear?" he asked.

"The truth," I said with all the bravery in my heart.

"Until I'm happy," he said. "That's the essence, right? You stop when you're not happy," he added.

Until. He's. Happy.

My heart crashed into a million pieces, and that's not poetry. I didn't know that anything could hurt that much. I didn't know anyone could love you so much only to walk away when he's no longer happy. I didn't know relationships are meant to end when happiness ceases to exist. I didn't know convenience was the centerpiece of a relationship.

I thought sacrifices and unhappiness were all part of this big picture we call relationships. I thought love meant to always try, even when it gets difficult and when the days aren't as comfy as they used to be. I thought love was hard work clothed in numerous efforts and abundant patience. I thought the purpose of relationships was to see if we can make it through the happy days and the horrible ones.

I didn't know you only wanted to live the happy days. I didn't know you only wanted to make this work when it was easy. I didn't know that you only wanted me when I caused happiness and that you would walk out when I'm being too heavy to deal with, when I'm magnified in my insecurities. I didn't know that the essence of building a life is only staying when it's all smiles and dinner dates and kisses and hugs. *I didn't know you only wanted this when it's all perfect. I guess I didn't know many things after all.*

And that's what I hoped I had the courage to tell you. But…

"Okay." That's what I said.

The Human Heart

It's disappointing how people don't see the entirety of a human heart, how beautiful and breathtaking it is. It's tragic how people don't see how amazing it is to have the opportunity to carry someone's heart in their own hands. It's sad how reckless people can be when it comes to human hearts. They don't see the magnitude and the force that can break free from it. They don't see how capable their hands are of smashing it and destroying it piece by piece. It's disheartening how people can just play around with it and take it for granted. They disregard how fragile a human heart can be and how much power they have for actually owning it in their own hands. They disrespect it and they don't shower it with enough gentleness and kindness, they just let it fall and break and then leave once it's broken and paralyzed and disabled, once it's messy and hard to care for.

When in all truth, they should be nurturing it, watering it so it will grow, giving it just enough light for it to be healthy. They should be making meaningful moments and even more meaningful conversations. They should be inspiring it to grow as beautiful as it can be and giving it the freedom to glow and pursue the things that makes them a better person. They should be making time for it, listening to it and providing enough encouragement and air to breathe, planting it in a really good soil, providing it the right amount of love and care, and granting it the space to rise up into the being they're supposed to be.

It's a lot of responsibility to hold a human heart, but you can't imagine how fulfilling it is to know that you were a part of its growth and development, that you were a mother to it—to a heart that is now even more spectacular.

65

First

I hated the fact that I wasted the idea of first love. I regret loving someone too much during the days that I was only learning to love. I wish I didn't waste much of my energy and emotion on someone else. I hope I didn't spend my early years loving people who are too difficult and too demanding to love and just focus on the idea of loving myself. Then maybe, I would have grown up continuously learning to accept and love myself more than I grew to love temporary connections.

The Problem With Us

The problem is we seek approval from others rather than ourselves. We listen to their opinion and we live in the walls of their validation. We open our hearts and we let their lies make their way into our hearts. We constantly do things to win their hearts and shrink ourselves every time we would feel bigger than them. We allow them to step on us and not rise above their lies.

The problem is we judge people and we make it a goal to change them, to have them fit our standards. Not realizing that we are all different and we all have distinct identity, we cannot change people. We cannot fix them, either; we can only accept them. And if we would start practicing that, we could lift an immense amount of pressure off of our shoulders. It can be nice to just live and know that we are accepted for who we are.

The problem is we crave glory. We do things, pursue goal after goal that doesn't really satisfy us. We do it in order to become somebody, not knowing that *that* life is empty. Unless we focus truly on the things we really want to do with our lives, we'll never live a full life.

The problem is more in who we let go than who we let stay. We let people slip away; we allow chances to escape. We never risk anything or lower our pride in order to keep people. We don't value the people who come in our lives; instead, we allow them to walk out.

The problem is that we are more critical than compassionate. We see the glitches more than we see the goodness. We like to discuss and scrutinize the shortcomings of other people; we like to discourage, we like to destroy. It's true. Instead of wasting our energy on being kind and marveling at the beauty in them—we see all the specks in their eyes and we insist that they remove them, that they be better versions of themselves when they are already wonderful to begin with, when we should be the ones bettering ourselves.

The problem is we always let fear take over. We get stuck in this idea that we want a safe, comfortable and undisturbed life. We turn away at the first sign of trouble, the first noise of danger; we run as fast as we can. We always fear. But life is a big adventure and we'll never really know that unless we go out there and experience it, facing our own fears. We need to learn to embrace life and all of its surprises. We need to stop being frightened of what might happen, what people might say; we just need to *be*. Be who we always long to be, soar higher than our own expectations *without any hint of fear. Just living, unapologetically.*

I Don't Want To Love You Too Much

To be honest, I don't want to love you too much. I don't want to love you like a crazy person. I don't want to love you with all my heart, with all my strength. I don't want to build my life upon you and have you complete the missing parts of me. I don't want to offer you all the love from this little body of mine. I don't.

Because if I do, I'm almost giving you all of me. And I don't want that.

I don't want to be the girl who loves too much and leaves nothing for herself. I'm scared. No, wait—I'm terrified. I don't want you walking away from that door taking everything that I am, taking every single piece of myself. I don't want you fleeing and leaving me with holes that were once so full of life. I don't want you gone from my life. I don't want to be the girl who has her life together before you and have it fall apart after you.

Goodness, I don't want that.

I want to be the girl who loves you just right, who leaves a fair amount of love for herself, who will know how to move forward when you're gone. The girl who will know how to heal, the girl who can cry and mend without you. I want to be the girl who loves herself more. I want to be able to stand on my own and be excited for myself, who can wake up whole.

And maybe it is brave to love someone so much to the point that you will give your whole being to them, unafraid. But you know what? I'm not that brave. I don't want to be that kind of brave.

I just want to be brave enough to leave portions of love for myself.

Brave enough to love people simultaneously as I love myself. I don't want to forget myself in the process of loving you. I don't want to take myself for granted—what I want, what I need and what my dreams are—I just want to be brave enough to remember myself.

68

The Universe Doesn't Want Us

I have loved people who didn't choose me,
people who constantly destroy me,
people who either leave me hurt, beaten, or ruined.
I have been with people who either make me question my worth
or change me so I'll fit them better.
And the moral is—
you leave and you don't settle.

So when you do find someone who is good to you,
who treats you with value and respect,
who loves you sincerely,
you want to hold on to that,
you *have* to hold on to that.
You want to keep that because it's not every day you find someone
just like that.

But sometimes
the universe wants to play,
and sometimes
you're bound to lose.

That I don't know how to deal with exactly,
because love has never been this good to me—
I want it to stay
but I guess the universe doesn't want it to.

69

Love Ends The Moment They Become Hard Work

Love ends when you allow the aches and the faults magnify. Love ends when the respect is gone, when you highlight the flaws, the shortcomings, and the weaknesses. Love ends the moment you start shutting them off, the moment you start saying you're exhausted, when patience and understanding is no longer a must but more like a duty. *Love ends when you stop trying.*

When You Leave

You leave them with a pile of doubts on whether or not they're good enough. You leave them wondering if they'll ever be worthy of someone's love. You leave them asking a series of questions, of 'why's, 'how's, 'what's. You leave them with an immense amount of desire to do it all over again, but this time, to actually do it differently. You leave them with a heart that apologizes for whatever they did that prompted you to leave. You leave them with desperate 'what if's—what if it worked out, what if you continue on, we could have been this, we could have been that. You leave them with so many scenarios filled with wishful thinkings. You leave them with non-stop re-runs of memories with hints of hope that there could have been more. You leave them with a huge hole in their chest, with a huge bruise that's almost impossible to restore.

You leave them with trauma. You leave them with pillows as wet as their eyes. You leave them with a heart that beats too fast and too hard it might explode. You leave them with sleepless, painful nights. Bearing all the longing and excruciating aches you caused. Suffering all the loneliness and tears you created.

You leave them with fear: fear of trusting, fear of giving in, fear of loving.

And that's permanent.
That's permanent.
You can never undo that.

71

I Always Miss You

Despite all the laughter and the tears,
you will always be the greatest thing that ever happened to me,
the one thing I wish I never lose,
the one thing I will always miss,
the one thing that will always be a part of me.
Come back, please.

You Weren't There

It was hard, and you weren't there.

You weren't there when things started to become rougher than they already had been. You weren't there when I felt like the world was crashing down on me. You weren't there when there wasn't a single thing I understood. You weren't there when I had no one to hold on to. You weren't there when sleeping at night was burdensome, when waking up was a battle on its own.

You weren't there when all I needed was you telling me that I can make it through, you comforting me with His promises, you assuring me that I will overcome and that you will be with me every step of the way, you lending me your shoulder and letting me cry on it for God knows how long. You weren't there when all I needed was to hear your voice. You weren't there when all I needed was your presence.

You weren't there when all I needed was you. You weren't there when all I ever wanted was you.

You weren't there.

And I can't blame you, so I'm sorry if I feel like this. If I feel like you're one of the best people in my life, if I feel like you're obligated to be there for me. I'm sorry if I expected too much from you.

You weren't there.

It was the toughest thing ever, but it was totally okay. Because in your absence, I learned that I am so much stronger than what I give myself credit for. I am so much braver than my overflowing fears. I am so much more capable than my weaknesses. In your absence, I knew I had to take on this challenge alone. I had to mourn alone. I had to grieve alone. I had to suffer alone. In your absence, I realized that I cannot really expect even the closest people to be there when I needed them most. I realized that people can veritably come and go, that friendships can die, friendships can hurt, friendships can be far away and not beside you when you so solely need them to be.

You weren't there.

And it verified one thing: at the darkest moment of our lives, even our shadows leave us. And if they do, it applies more so for people. That you may not be there when I am waging the most arduous war of my life. But you taught me to stand firm on my own. You directed me to be my own refuge, to be my own hero, to be my own comfort. You taught me to never put my whole trust in you and to never expect so much from you, from people in general. Because people will disappoint. You will disappoint. Because it'll hurt. It hurts now.

You weren't there. And that taught me that I can do it. I can overcome, not with you, but with myself.

Choice

And how can two people who used to love each other deeply—who used to just stay over the phone, not saying anything but just hearing each other breathe, how two people who used to spend as much time together and still couldn't get enough—look at each other with so much angst and hate?

After being in love for a while, that's when it will hit you: staying in love is something you choose. It's not a matter of chance, it's a choice. Love dies when you stop choosing it. When you start choosing all the things you hate about each other—all the annoying stuff they do, all the pain and damage they caused you—instead of choosing love. Instead of choosing forgiveness and second chances, instead of choosing the good memories, the hugs, the affection. Instead of *choosing each other.*

74

As If

She came back—
And you run as fast as you can
Thinking of all the possibilities
and the chances that were not given before,
you thought of all the things you could've been,
how you can start over
and build a life worth living
a relationship worth all the effort,
like you can begin again;
a fresh start.

And as soon as you reached her,
you held her
so tight that nothing could ever come between the both of you,
and you kissed her as if you were kissing an angel
and you gazed at her—
as if I didn't exist,
as if you couldn't hear the very sound of my heart breaking,
and my hope crashing,
as if you didn't promise me loyalty
and love
and future;
as if I wasn't there,

as if her coming back was
'meant to happen'.

75

Deep

Maybe the problem is my memories are deep,
open me and see all the ache I keep
bleeding as if
I just reap.

76

Most Definitely

Maybe he isn't as magnificent as he appears to be.
Maybe he's just some boy,
some desperate,
lonely boy
you can unlove.

Some awful,
insensible boy
you can forget.

All Of The Above

The medicines might've killed you,
or the tubes, the non-stop nurses' rounds,
the tube they pushed through your throat to give you oxygen
without realizing it may be the same thing that can take it away,
the incalculable injections,
the liquids that made your body weaker and weaker,
thinner and thinner.

Or all of that, perhaps.
They took the light,
the hope, the life;
they took you
when they should've made you stayed.

When You Stop Loving Me

I know it will come—maybe next month or after a few years—but when it does come, and you will approach me with sad eyes and a heart that is as heavy as your breath, I will listen. I will listen to every word you will speak; I will be strong, I will be courageous and I will just listen. No matter how much it will destroy every fiber of my being, no matter how words like 'I don't love you anymore' woven with tears and a shaking voice will put a solid rock in my chest, I will just listen.

I can't promise you I won't cry, though. I might—no—*I will*. And I won't be able to control my tears as they flow like a wild river. But I will accept; I will swallow every word with tenderness, I will embrace your goodbye and all the reasons behind it with understanding.

And I will let you go. I will allow you to leave. I will open the door and I will wave my hand with a smile, because no matter how diffi-cult it will be for me, no matter how broken I will be, I wouldn't drag you down with me. I wouldn't sacrifice your future happiness and the joy that is waiting for you out there just so I can fulfill my own selfish desires. I won't steal your chances at finding a better love than me; I won't snatch your hope and your freedom just because I love you too much and I want you for myself.

I will be a train wreck when that time comes. And if I'm being com-pletely honest, I don't know how I will put myself back together, how I will gather all the pieces of my broken heart and how I will build my life back up and running—oh God, I have no idea. I will be a dis-aster. But I will be happy for you, I will be glad and grateful for what we had, for our time together, for all the memories and the promises, for the good times and the hard ones, as well. I will be glad that you have found your new joy, whether it is in the face of your career, your freedom, your family, your passion or in someone new—I will be truly happy for you.

And if you ever think of me, maybe one night when you're in your bed alone and you might miss me, know that I will be here waiting for you. If life or love comes and breaks you, come to me and I will do my best to help you heal. Come to me, back to me, because I will always wait for you. I will leave the keys under the rug like we used to, I will leave the lights on, I will wait. I will always wait.

Part 3

The Aftermath

Forgetting Is A Choice

The world doesn't owe you healing. Time doesn't owe you mending. You have to choose it. You have to channel every ounce of strength left inside you and turn that into forgetting. You have to face the ocean and with much wildness and bravery, say your goodbye. Wash away all the sand in your hair. Unlearn every surging and plunging, every spilling and collapsing of the waves. You have to stop being familiar with the heat. You have to cover every burn, bind every scorch. You have to erase every feeling, every memory of what it's like being in it. Being with *them*. You have to look at the sky and think different things. You have to leave every taste, every melody, every sight. You have to remember other things. You have to help yourself. You have to drag yourself out of the ocean and into a new discovery, into a new adventure. The rays and waves won't help you forget; the wind and the sand won't help you rinse every piece they left. You have to do your part, cure every broken fragment, fill every inch of the cracks, surround every hole. You have to do it, you just have to do it.

How You Grow

You don't bloom when other people struggle
when they go all out
and hurt themselves
and bleed

You bloom when *you* struggle
when the waves hit you but you keep rising
when the tears keep falling but you keep smiling
when the rain keeps pouring but you keep going
when the war is almost over but you keep fighting

you bloom when you are bruised
and crushed
but you choose to grow flowers in all the broken spots.

Let This Be The Time You Will Finally Heal

The year you will rise above every heartache, sorrow, and loss. The year you will mend every battle scar and open wound. The year you will gather all the broken pieces of your heart, of your soul, of your life, and put them together and bandage every crack until they become whole again. Let this be the year you will realize that it's okay to be broken, to cry, and to grieve, but it's not okay to stay like that forever. Let this year be a year of hope, assurances that there will be better days for you, that there is a joy set before you after all this mourning. That the sun will rise and the storm will cease, and the aftermath will not be as messy as the calamity but it will be beautiful, it will be glorious. Let this year be the year you will realize that the ruins are magnificent. Let this year be a year of utter healing. Healing of every physical, mental, emotional, and spiritual pain and suffering. A year of regaining all the lost strength and courage, a year of admittance—that we are broken, that we need healing. A year of just taking your time to heal, no matter how slowly, as long as you are healing. A year you will no longer fake strength but just be honest with what's going on inside you. Let this year be the year you will be whole again.

Let this be the time you will redeem yourself. The year you will recover from everything that damaged you in the past from every defeat, every pang of pain, every wave of weeping, every single thing that wrecked you. Let this be a magical year where you will reclaim yourself and wind up above all these things. Let this year be the year you will boldly walk on water, knowing who you are and what you're made of. Defying all kinds of limits and overcoming whatever life will throw at you.

Let this be the time you will realize that you are created to survive.

82

I Am Becoming

and I'm not even sorry I am
because really this is not an overnight job
this was 22 years in the making
crafted with heartaches and sorrow
with nothingness and fullness
all together

I am,
I am becoming.

If This Life Has Taught Me Anything Valuable, It's This

You can do everything and will still find it impossible to chase after people who doesn't want to be chased.

And don't tell me I've learned this from one fallen relationship—I've learned this from so many people who have graced my life, only to leave after quite some time. I've learned this from so many people that have won my heart and attached their soul to mine only to leave like nothing happened, like it wasn't such a big deal that I have invested so much of myself and my time in them. I've learned this from so many people who built strong relationships with me only to build stronger walls between us. I've learned this from so many people who walked in only to walk out when things got tougher telling me that time could fix shit.

Let me tell you, it will hurt. It will hurt really bad. Like the world is breaking up with you and the waves are surging and you have no choice but to drown. It hurts. But one thing is for sure, you are firmer and greater than this. You're resilient enough to pull yourself together and bold enough to let go. Let them go. I repeat, *let them go.*

As you allow them the space to be who they want to be and be with the people they want to be with, you will find within you the courage to accept that people do come and go. That you need to just breathe and rest in the fact that you cannot *keep* everyone you love. Some connections will really fall apart, friendships will crash, people will outgrow each other, and that's just how life is.

Above all this, know that you will grow and you will evolve and you will find your people and you will craft relationships that will last longer than you.

Let go.

84

But Look At You Now

You've grown with your burns,
stretch marks, battle scars, and imperfections—
all of which only made you one of a kind
and more beautiful than you already are.

Refuge

After everything, believe that you have built your being into something that can never be destroyed by anything or anyone. You have supported your art, regardless of how many people tell you you're not doing any good. You have guarded your heart, taking it away from the hands of those who refuse to swim in its depth. You have protected your beliefs, even when you are left alone; even when nobody believes in you, you stood like a mountain. You have molded your being into something that can never be shaken; no matter how many catastrophes hit and go, you remained still.

You fought for your life, for your soul, and for your heart. You took courage and became your own refuge. And that's good, because really, no one will fight for you like you do.

86

War

She didn't wake up to be pretty,
she woke up to make war
and vanquish her own demons.

Little Reminders

It's always easier to condemn yourself. For all the wrong things you've done, for the times you lost control, for the mistakes, the undesirable past. It's always easier to belittle yourself and believe that you're not good for anything, not meant for incredible, extraordinary things. It's always easier to take note of the things you're lacking, the reasons why you will always fall in the minimum. It's always easier to tell yourself bad things that for a while may sound harmless but really in the long run, you're only damaging yourself more, deeper. It's always easier to declare things that won't allow you to rise up and defeat the wind in your sail. It's always easier to just accept the fact that you won't ever be magnificent.

Today, kindly look at yourself and look at all your scars, all your cuts; those are silent and gentle reminders that you are overcoming, that you are destroying your own demons, that you are sailing well. Be reminded of all your calluses and your battered knees; that is evidence of the numerous mountains you have successfully shrunk so you can reach the top. Be reminded of all your pain and heartaches and griefs and know that those are the proofs that you're alive, that you are walking on the waters and taking control of your own journey. Those are only tiny reminders that you are, little by little, overcoming. Let these things be enough reasons for you to move more mountains and walk through more seas and set sail even in the strongest of winds. *Let these things be a magnificent reminder that you can.*

88

Bolder

For the longest time I craved approval
of my choices, of my actions
of who I love, of what I do
when I should only be considering
one voice.
Even He allows me to hit rock bottom
and make mistakes,
not to hurt me, but to mold me
into someone firmer,
someone bolder.

On Loving Yourself

What if the love you deserve is not distant? What if the love you deserve doesn't come from a perfect lover? What if it comes from yourself? What if you just have to walk yourself home after a long day and treat yourself to coffee and just find love in the serenity of it all? What if you just have to take yourself to magnificent places around the world and bask in the beauty of being whole on your own? What if you just have to hold your hand when it gets disturbing at night and pat your own back and whisper words like "It's gonna be okay. *You're* gonna be okay."? What if you just have to be fearless enough to find fullness in yourself and have the guts to stick with it through joy, insecurity, and depression? What if you just have to be satisfied with all your shortcomings and be assured that you are trying, that you are capable, that you are sufficient. What if in the end of it all you just you have to find all the remaining pieces of yourself from places, experiences, developments, and endeavors and mend them all back together and finish a beautiful masterpiece that is *you*.

No Matter

His promises will come through. His love will surpass all your circumstances. His peace will fill your heart. His grace will wash away your tears. His compassion will forgive your shortcomings. You are made for far grander things. Your future is saturated with hope and joy. Everything you touch, every ground you walk on, will prosper. You are walking on holy ground; the entire track of your life is breakthrough. *You need to just trust His process.*

91

Moving On

You can't just move on from people. It's a process. It's days that turn into months and months that turn into years. It's scrubbing and peeling. It's washing and crying. It's longing and loving. It's waiting and hurting. It's dying while breathing.

To My Younger Self

And if you ask me what I would tell my younger self, first of all, I would tell her to fight, to be bold enough in all situations, to never back down from any strife. I would tell her that her soul is made up of fire and her heart is made up of stars, and with them she's expected to be blazing with brightness. I would tell her that life is difficult but surely she will brave an infinite number of oceans and she will only get better in time. I would tell her to always be firm on her choices, to never let anyone tell her who she is because she knows exactly who she is. I would tell her to be relentless in the pursuit of the things that make her heart beam. I would tell her that her dreams aren't bigger than her because they're absolutely not; she can and she will, she will achieve everything she sets her heart and mind into. I would tell her to always, always love—because really, it's the most astounding feeling in the world. Lastly, I would tell her she's a survivor, because she is.

All The Things I'm Not
And All The Things I Am

After years and years of hating myself and endlessly denouncing all the parts I dislike and adoring only the fraction I can bear, I eventually grew weary.

I learned that I will always be dirty, clumsy, and ugly. I will always have stretch marks around my thighs, dark circles around my eyes, and maybe extra fat in my belly. I will always have my fair share of scars and wounds. I will always be drowning in blemishes and glitches. I will never be enough for everybody, neither will I be easy.

There will be times when I'll give people a hard time. Days I'll say sorry more times than I should and explain myself over and over again just to make sure the people I love understand. Times I'll try harder than I should, ask more questions than what's required. Moments I'll be too big to handle. Instances where I'll overthink the hell out of my mind, where I'll be too emotional to deal with, with a heart too enormous to carry. There will always be occasions that I won't be at my best; I will be a mess.

And over time, I have learned to love it. I have loved every curve, every nook and cranny, every edge, every rhythm, every aspect of who I am, of what I do, of my abilities and disabilities. I have learned to harness all the energy I use to hate myself and transform it to positive energy, devoting every ounce of it to accepting myself, loving every fraction of myself. I learned to love all the appalling parts of me, all my infirmities. The way I move, the way I love, the way I do things, the way I treat people, I learned to fondle every single element of my humanness. I learned to love myself through the most atrocious of days and the most favorable of days, through my sloppiness and openness. I learned to love it all.

I learn to love myself with forgiveness, all the things that I'm not and of all the things that I am.

I Stopped Listening

I always listen.

I made it a habit to always listen to what people tell me, their advice, critiques, and opinions. I always listen and sometimes I can't control it anymore. I become a sponge. I let all their words in, I am drenched in every letter and drowning myself in every sentence; I let it all penetrate in my heart.

And that's the problem—I don't have my own voice. I get so caught up with what they want for me, what they think is right for me. I can never stand up for anything because I easily get swayed by voices, and most of the time I can't even hear my own voice.

I lose my control, I lose my foothold. I lose my heart and I just nod. I can't decide on my own anymore. I let them influence my very core. Without a word, I do whatever they want me to do, be whomever they need me to be. However, they won't take account for my actions. They will never feel responsible for what becomes of me.

I am in charge of myself.

What I do, who I am, who I love, how I'll be happy, what job I take, what interest I pursue, what passion I feed—I will be the one suffering the consequences of my decisions and mistakes. I will be held accountable for whatever mess I create in my life. I will be the one singing with joy or the one crying in the rain. The one celebrating or the one who is afflicted. The bottom line is that no matter what they tell me, it's up to me. Everything is ultimately up to me. I can set and live on my own terms. I can filter their words, their opinions, and maybe lower down their volume a little bit.

And you can do the same. You are your own person. Don't let every-thing they say make its way into your heart. Don't let the lies inflict you, let it fall by the curb. Don't let it bother you and confuse you about everything you ever believed in.

You set your beliefs, your standards. You set your own tone, your own pace, and you run your way. Because when all is said and done, it's you who's going to be in your room one night thinking of all these and regretting why you listened too much, why you did not filter, why you saturated yourself with their opinions and why you get too affected, and why you didn't care at all about what you think or what you felt.

It's you who's going to sink deeply into regrets. It's you who'll find it hard to sleep because you're occupied with 'what if's—What if you listened to yourself a little more? What if you spoke a little louder and let your own voice overcome the noises? What if you chose your-self?—then maybe your life would be a little brighter now. *And honey, when that time comes, I hope it's not too late.*

To Remain Wildly In Love

I want us to be certain. I don't want us to look forward to broken relationships and believe in pain and suffering and breaking more than we believe in the magnitude of our love. I don't want us saying things like 'it's inevitable' or 'it's supposed to happen'. I don't want ambiguity; too many things and people in my life are already unsure of whether or not they'll stay. You, however—I want to be sure. I want you to be sure of your affection, of your feeling, of your heart—for me.

I want us to always try. I don't want us to be lax. I want us to always set the ground we walk on on fire. To always exert the extent of our efforts. I want you to know that this will work, that this isn't another petty come-and-go relationship. I want us to make a huge impact in each other's lives. I want us to make wonders and joy out of this relationship.

I want us to be firm, that we will fight for this, as much as we can. That we will always choose each other. That love will always be greater than any frustration, argument, or fight. That at the end of the day, we will not sweep it under the rug or shake it off, we will communicate and we will make sure we are honest about how we feel, with our pain, and everything else in between. That before we go to sleep at night, we know our hearts are pure, not hating nor counting, but having everything out there in the open.

I want us to be careful. I don't want us to destroy each other when a specific period reaches us. I don't want us going around slamming doors in each other's faces and calling each other names, yelling all the things we did for each other as if we owe it to one another; I don't want that. I don't want all of this to be the focus of our once lovely relationship.

I want us to build each other in love, in gratefulness, in gentleness, in patience, and in kindness. I want us to know the value and the significance of the love we have. I want us to realize that this is important, that it's not every day we find a love like this, that this is bewildering in its ordinariness. I want us to comprehend the idea that we have each other, and that we once fell totally hard in love, that there were things and traits we found in each other that are very much striking and beautiful—let that be enough reason why we wouldn't want to lose each other.

Most of all, I want us choose to love. I want us to wrap our minds around how real this is and how amazing it is to find someone who's not scared to love us back, who's brave in pursuing us, who's willing to take the risk of getting hurt, who's going out of their way to make us feel loved and wanted, who reassures us every single day how worthy we are, who knows their priorities and is willing to make this last. I want us to hold this as tightly as we can. I want us to remain beautifully, wildly in love because this is real. *This is real.*

96

Survivor

It's startling how people survive. How they're not made up of gold and their bones aren't bred out of iron but still they seem like it. There's so much beauty on how they rise really.

So, honey, next time you think you won't survive or that you're weak, or you just can't do it—just rest in certainty and grace that survival is possible. Survival is real. I've seen it.

I've seen people who fought, people who rose as life constantly beat them down. I've seen people who lost mothers, people who bled, people who never felt the shine of the sun but still hoped and persevered. I've seen people rose from the most devastating catastrophes, so I don't see why you can't.

You can. Because every time I would look at you—I see strength. I see you stand tall before all your circumstances. I see you find all the healing you need. I see the possibility of restoration. I see you gather pieces of yourself and put it back together gently. I see you and I see hope, grit, and resilience, but most of all, I see a survivor.

There's Healing

If I am being completely honest, it took me a long time to realize that the world is not out there to get me, it's not out there to damage me, it's not out there to offer me more heartaches, it's not out there to cause any havoc, *it's just there.*

When I began to look at the world through a different lens, that's when I realized that there's empathy and forgiveness out there. And the world is actually filled with gentleness and humanity.

I began to find healing from the places I set my foot into. From every foreign land and distinct culture, from every fresh morning breeze down unfamiliar streets. I experienced healing from every new face I encountered, from every dialect and accent I'd never heard before. I experienced healing in wave after wave of islands I visited for the first time and in every whisper of mountains whose summit I got to reach.

I found healing through experiences. Through every rising and falling. I experienced healing through each tear that ever fell from my eyes; I experienced healing in every hurt, in every laughter. I experienced healing through every victory and every loss, in every chance and situation I found myself in, in every learning process; in every chapter of my life. I looked closely and all I see was healing.

I found healing in the people I met. I experienced healing through every late-night conversation over coffee, knowing that I was not alone in life. I experienced healing through every weekend getaway with the people that built me up in love and inspired me to keep going; I experienced healing in the simplest 'hello, how are you?'

from people I knew and even those I didn't. I experienced healing through every single connection I ever made, in every kiss, every hug, every gaze, and every touch. I experienced healing through the lives of the people who came across my path with their own struggles, their own process, through the people who pated my back, people who held me with carefulness.

And most of all, I found healing in admitting the fact that we all need it. That we all can offer it and that we must. *For healing's sake. For our sakes.*

98

May We All Heal

however we can.
And may we all survive
however we can
because we can
we can.

99

Saving

In every trial there's a way. In every situation there's a silver lining. In every sin there's forgiveness. In every fault there's a solution. In every hurt there's mending. In every struggle there's triumph. In every hardship there's a lesson. In every fear there's freedom. In every limitation there's grace. In every battle there's saving.

In this life, you really don't need to be hard on yourself. We all stumble, we all break, we all fall apart. The important thing is that we hope—in all these things. We hope in life, in the fact that wherever we are right now, mountain high or valley low, there's saving. *There is saving.*

100

To You

I hope you take a closer look at your heart today. I hope you finally realize that you deserve forgiveness, you deserve to call it quits and let go of all that's weighing you down, all the things that make you feel heavy and hurt. I hope you forgive yourself for all the lack, for all the faults, for all the wrong things you have done. I hope you finally realize that you deserve a life more than self-condemnation and self-judgment. I hope you see how fragile and soft you are, how you break at times and how you're not perfect, how you fall short. I hope you realize that it's okay—because you are a human being. You are supposed to make mistakes and fight, you are supposed to fail and learn afterward; it's all about how you move forward. With that, I hope you also find it in you to realize that you deserve kindness—be kind to yourself. Know that you are trying, always trying, and sometimes that's more than enough.

Moving Forward

At the end of the day, you deserve the life you've always longed for. You deserve to obtain your heart's desire. For one, you don't deserve to settle for a mediocre life. You deserve to live a life smoldering with passion and spirit. A life that is woven from your own ambitions. You deserve to live that life—so rise up, exert effort, do what you must in order to achieve that life. Because if you don't make a move, you won't get there. You deserve it, but the world will not hand it over to you. You have to get up, conquer your own Goliath, climb your own mountains, and sail your own stormy seas. At the end of it all, when you get there, I promise you that it will be worth it.

This Is Me Starting Over

This is me acknowledging every single opportunity I screwed up, every single occasion I disappointed those dear to me; this is me realizing how bad I muddled things, how I dragged people with me, how I burned people, and how I definitely failed.

This is me feeling bad about every wrong choice I made. Every time I let the urge of making a mistake be stronger than making things right, every time my willpower and conviction wasn't enough, for every moment I didn't stand unshakeable, every moment I was only being swayed by the flow. This is me feeling bad about every sin, every fault.

This is me realizing that I am human. That I also need to be patient with myself; that there is still mercy and second chances. This is me realizing that I need to give myself more than just burdens and problems. This is me understanding that I need to let go of the past; I need to set myself free from my own toxic expectations. I need to forgive myself for all the times I wasn't enough, for all the times I didn't make it.

This is me in total candor that I often fail. But this is also me encouraging myself to start over. To give it one more shot—this time with much boldness and strength, with more conviction and determination.

This is me trying again. This is me starting over again.

103

I Refuse To Break My Spine

and bend my bones
and stretch my skin
for people who wouldn't even
break a nail—
no,
not for me.

Looking At Life In A Different Light

Today is different.

Not like any other day when I would look at my life and make myself believe that I am stuck. I am uninspired and desperately, relentlessly going around in circles. On most days, I would allow myself to believe a series of lies that my life won't get any better. I would continue down this tunnel and convince myself that I had reached the light at the end. I question if there will still be progress, if I can ever move forward from where I am. *And that's not doing myself any favors.*

Today, I convince myself to just breathe.

I persuade myself to stand assured that God is in control, that I am exactly where I am meant to be today. I tell myself to open my eyes and see life in a different light, to see my tears as blessings, to see my disappointments and defeats as a sign of promise, as a plan that is grander than what I can ever comprehend. I tell myself to be still because He will reveal all to come. I tell myself to just be, guaranteed and ensured that He is God, even though I can't understand every single thing all at once. He is a God whose thoughts are higher than mine, a God who'll finish all He has begun.

Today, I declare confidence.

I allow myself to just be bold in Him and trust in the fact that He is reigning over my life. That all of these rejections and this heaviness is just temporary, because there's truth in His promises. I am meant for far brighter things. But not in my own time—in His time. And wherever He has me right now, whether it is the darkest or the lowest point, I am secured. He's never failing and I will stand in His victory.

Today, I teach myself to be grateful.

I grant myself the space to just appreciate whatever I have and keep going to wherever He is leading me, whatever He is doing. Regardless of if waking up feels too much already, regardless of if I feel like the whole universe has turned its back on me; regardless of if I feel like I'll never be accepted anywhere, like I will always be deficient, regardless of if I feel like I'll never move forward.

Today, I train my mind and my eyes to stop looking at the temporary things.

I stop fixating on this world with its limitations and impossibilities. I stop concentrating on the things I can do, things I can't do, my capabilities, and my circumstances. I just look at my life with courage, embrace every single frustration, every single hurt with patience and belief that things will fall in place.

Today, I know.

I am sure of Him. Everything else is uncertain, and that's how things will always be; we cannot control everything. Our future in Him is incontestable; things will get better, they always do. In every struggle there will be a breakthrough. He is a faithful God, and all these lies, all these things that we permit to sabotage us from the inside out, He will use these very things to strengthen our faith and deliver us.

There Is No Shame In Being Needy

I don't understand why we waste an awful amount of energy trying to be self-reliant, trying to be our own heroes. And when we look closely, we can see how impaired we are and how we deteriorate. We often think that we are broken beyond repair. We look closer and see hopelessness. We embrace our mistakes and sins as if they were meant to live within the depths of our bones, as if we cannot be better than that, as if there's no recovering.

In our attempt not to drag people down with us, we are just hurting all the more. Our scars, aches, shortcomings, frailties—they just intensify. We lodge in self-pity, in damnation. And the worst thing is that we hide it; we don't allow anyone to see even the slightest hint of what we're going through, not even the glimpse of our bruises. We walk around feeling like we're alone in this battle, like nobody could ever wrap their minds around whatever we are going through. The heaviness and the numbness just grows and grows.

But get this—there is no shame in being needy.

There is absolutely nothing wrong in going through whatever we're going through, and most especially, we need to understand that we are never alone. We can reach out. We can open ourselves up to those around us, to the world. Because sometimes our biggest enemy is ourselves, and the prison we need to release ourselves from *is* ourselves, and the ultimate person we need to forgive is ourselves. *We need to let ourselves go and be needy, once and for all.*

It Was Almost Impossible To Wash Away Every Memory

...to erase every trace and come out clean and new, I know. The scent feels as if they were engraved on your bones, the way their kisses taste and how their hands feel at the sides of your waist; it will always feel like they're still there. As if their hands are glued to your waist and their lips are on your lips. Their outspoken ideas and fascinating experiences feel like they're woven within your being, as if it was your very own. The joy and the sense of loving them and being loved by them is pure bliss and pure pain and it stains. It leaves a huge blot you can't wipe out smoothly, I know.

And as you try to scrape it all away, you noticed you are only punishing yourself, tormenting yourself all the more. You noticed how difficult it is, especially when it feels like you're peeling away your own skin. Especially when you are trying to sort and separate pieces of yourself and only keep what is easy to bear and then throwing away the pieces that cause anguish. It's difficult when all of these pieces have already found a home within the depths of your body, mind, and heart. And you realize that at the end of it all, erasing and scraping everything off piece by piece does not help you; it does not set you free. But making an effort to live with them—embracing each lesson, experience, feeling and everything else in between—actually does.

Because really, when it's all over, maybe letting go isn't really throwing the pieces away but using these pieces to strengthen you and mold you into a more beautiful version of yourself. Don't you think?

I'm Starting To Feel Like I'm Writing Myself In All The Wrong Stories Lately

I'm barking up all the wrong trees, shoving myself in all the wrong places, trying to shrink in order to fit where I don't belong.

But over time, I eventually learn to just let things take their own course. I learn to grant myself peace.

I learn to stop forcing life in a direction it's not meant to go. I learn to stop pressuring myself whenever I don't have the answers or whenever I don't know where I'll go or whenever I feel like I'm nowhere near my desires.

I learn to just let things be. Let things happen at their own pace, by their own design, and not try to manipulate things as much as I can. I learn to just rest and be at peace with all my worries and doubts. I learn to just be guaranteed that whatever is happening in my life has its reason, and sometimes I just have to allow it all to happen and not try to make it happen on my own way and my own timing. I learn to just let life be life.

I learn to just let the wind blow and the sun rise and the rain fall and the world move. I allow myself to wake up and live the life I have with peace and understanding that I do not need to rush anything, that I am certainly where I am meant to be at this very moment.

I learn to hold on to this peace. More than any wealth in the world, more than any job title, more than anything—for this peace holds everything still.

And sometimes, all I need is for everything to be still.

Let Them Love You First

Here's the thing: don't be so busy falling in love with everyone you meet. Instead, allow them to get to know you, to dig deeper into your soul, to understand who you really are, what you like, what you dislike, what makes your heart race, what makes your heart nervous. Let them comprehend why you value your family so much, why *NSYNC songs make you nostalgic, why you like Matcha over Espresso, why you'd rather walk than spend money on a cab. Open the door to your soul in order for them to understand why the smell of rain makes you giddy, why hugs are such a comfort, and why you fancy long talks when you're upset after a bad day at work. Give them the chance to sink into the reasons behind your every 'no', the success story behind every 'yes' and the tales behind every smile, every tear, every scar, every bruise, every trauma, every depression, every fear, every anxiety, every ache. Let them know every single inch of your soul.

At the same time, understand them, as well. Trace every emotion. Discover every secret they try so hard to keep. Explore why they're scared of opening up to people and why they cannot trust anyone in. Unearth the 'why's behind their favorite season: autumn, behind their favorite movie line: "Get busy livin' or get busy dyin'" from *Shawshank Redemption,* behind their favorite restaurant. Uncover the excuses why thunder scare them, why falling in love is threatening, and why they are the way they are.

If they willingly decided to love you, they will love you and they will be extremely sure of it. And you? *Honey, you'll race them to the finish line.*

109

May You Find It Within You

to let go
of all the things
you thought
you would be

You Wouldn't Know

…that pain killers could actually diminish pain unless your head is pounding and rest could not keep it still anymore. You wouldn't know that anti-depressants could ease depression for a while unless you're in your room at 1 AM, roughly at the edge, feeling too helpless. You wouldn't know agony unless you give yourself to people who wouldn't hold you with responsibility, unless you hand your heart to people who would not take good care of it. You wouldn't know heartbreak could absolutely wreck you until you fall in love with someone who insists they love you only to leave you in the cold. You wouldn't know healing was difficult unless you're alone, questioning your worth and all the reasons why you weren't deserving of their love. But you also wouldn't know how much of a survivor you are unless you realize that you are still here, reading this book, overcoming. *You're strong enough.*

111

Breakthrough

We need to be reminded that there's no shame in being needy, in being weak, in suffering from anxiety and depression, in admitting that we fear, that we doubt. We need to be reminded that we're all fighting and conquering our own oceans. We're all in this journey to overcome. And we need to be reminded that we will overcome, that we will have our deliverance, for our God is for us; He is never against us. Ultimately, we need to be reminded whose children we are.

112

What You Can See Right Now

…are just tragically beautiful reminders
of the mountains you moved,
the oceans you swam,
and the catastrophes you endured.
You have won.

113

Finding Yourself Takes Time

You have to unlearn every single thing people told you you are. You have to destroy every wall and discard every expectation. Finding yourself means washing away every foreign voice and peeling every influence off like an old skin. And it's difficult; it's a hard task, but trust me when I say that finding yourself is the greatest favor you can ever do for yourself.

114

Arriving At Life

I honestly feel like I'm always waiting for my life to happen. I'm always in the process of delaying my plans and dreams just because I feel like it's not yet time. Because there will be more soon. That I will arrive at a life one day where everything will be okay, everything will be put together, that every single piece of my life will be in the exact place it is meant to be. And that, by far, is the biggest lie I ever made myself believe.

I don't have much time. The only thing I am and we all are very much sure of is the fact that we are here—alive, breathing, and capable thinkers. Second is the fact that we will die one day. Everything else in between—we are not sure. The time, the day, our age, or if we are able to fulfill our dreams, if we are able to push through our plans before we even exit this world, we don't know that. What we do know is that we have control; we have a choice over everything else in between. We can choose to either allow life to pass us by as if we're the audience of our own life, as if were just given free passes to watch it all as it goes down, OR alter it, rewrite it, start over if necessary. Because the truth is that we are the writers, the directors, the crew—we are all in it, in total control of our lives.

Thus, I choose to rewrite my life. I will no longer waver like I'm watching the stars, like something big and miraculous will happen in my life. Like I'll be going to a certain place of comfort and victory before I even realize that this is my life, the life I should live, the life I should pursue with quality. Because another crude truth is that whatever I have now, whoever I'm with now, wherever I am now, may be the highlight of my life. This may be as good as it gets, and if I fail to appreciate it and look at it with gentleness, I will fail to be joyful. I will fail to live a meaningful, happy life.

And let me tell you, it sucks to always want things. To always desire for more, to always think that we're lacking in life—it just weighs us down and will never push us or set us on a higher ground. It will just allow us to stay exactly where we are, drowning in inconsequential aspirations, dragging us even lower and lower, down on our knees. What we have now is all we have. Our time might be short. Our resources might be inadequate, but this may be everything.

Furthermore, whether we like it or not, this is our life. It's really up to us if we will pursue our dreams now, if we will make our passion our way of life, if we will spend our money for and with the people we love, if we will cherish our time as our kids grow up, if we will live a life that is worth every second of it. A life that is bred out of love, meaning, and quality, a life that is overwhelming with grace and kindness. Or we'll just wait for a certain time and a specific place; maybe we wait for a retirement fund until we start spending some significant time with our family, or maybe stand by for a promotion before we start taking care of ourselves, before figuring out that we also deserve some pampering even once in a while, even a little. Maybe we're waiting for a certain age for us to know that it is time to get serious or to fulfill our heart's desire, whether it is getting married, building a life or utterly quitting a job that no longer contributes to our being.

Whatever it is, the question is: will we always stick around feeling stuck and anticipating life? In reality, life is here. It's not something we'll arrive at. It's something we have to work on every single day because it's happening—right before our very eyes.

115

Maybe We Can't Really Imagine

Maybe we can't really imagine how God reaches out to us and how His grace covers even the darkest gaps of our being. Maybe we will never truly wrap our minds around how deep His grace is—and it's not just saving grace, it's also the sanctifying kind; it forgives over and over and over again. Maybe that's enough encouragement today to come home to Him and start over and be restored.

116

I Am Grateful

For one, God has never left me empty handed. God always comes forth, through the drought, through the storm. His blessings, provisions, and promises always seem to find me whether I am on mountain tops or in valleys. Not by my timing, but assuredly by His. And for that, dear God, **I am grateful.**

117

But I Want To Be Strong

not for myself
but for those around me.
I want to be on fire
not to burn others,
but to set them ablaze as well
so together we will burn
brighter than ever before.

118

In The End

what's meant for us
will come find us.

Thank You

I can't tell you how glad I am today, knowing that you have experienced every pain and every joy with me. With that, I would love to send my love to you and thank you. For reading this, for finishing my heart's words with tenderness; you are wonderful. May you keep fighting and surviving. May you shower those around you with love and kindness. May you be a light that shines, a light that can never be dimmed. I do hope it encouraged you, for I want nothing more than for this little book to be an instrument of inspiration.

To everyone who has walked me through this and helped me finish this little book—gratefulness and love, as well.

To Alex, who made a way for me—thank you for helping me through the process; you've been very amazing!

To my mother & Xander—you're my fire; you're both beyond spectacular. All this is for you. And to Ison—your art is magnificent, your soul is art, and you have inspired me a lot.

And lastly, to every single soul who became my inspiration as I draft every single page—you may know who you are or not, but needless to say, every single one of you has become my rock. Continue to be a light for people like me, your spirits have embolden me. I can't thank you all enough.

All glory and honor be to You, my King, for all this are only made possible through You.

Again, from the deepest corner of my heart, thank you.

About the Author

Dian is a writer from the Philippines. As soon as she began writing, she discovered just how fulfilling the experience is. Since then, she became unconditionally in love with how words can fearlessly express the deepest parts of oneself and how words can connect even the farthest hearts making being human a lot easier.

Through writing, she has found beauty in every single circumstance in life, how the most tragic occasions can become the most fascinating form of art. Through writing, she became a better person.

Dian wants nothing more than for her writings to resonate with the people around her and to be a vessel of inspiration one way or another. She hopes that her personal struggles can be a light for others.

She hopes to experience more in order to create more.

YOU MIGHT ALSO LIKE:

Seeds Planted in Concrete
by Bianca Sparacino

Your Soul is a River
by Nikita Gill

Bloom
by Shani Jay

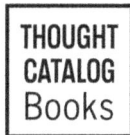

THOUGHT
CATALOG
Books

THOUGHT CATALOG

IT'S A WEBSITE.
www.thoughtcatalog.com

SOCIAL
facebook.com/thoughtcatalog
twitter.com/thoughtcatalog
tumblr.com/thoughtcatalog
instagram.com/thoughtcatalog

CORPORATE
www.thought.is